CONTENTS

About the Author v

Chapter 1 Getting started...1
   Introduction 1
   Why podcasts?...3

Chapter 2 It All Starts With You..7
   Part 1. Your goal 7
   Part 2. Finding your voice 11
   Part 3. Passion for what you do..14

Chapter 3 Finding the perfect podcasts for your business… 18
   Part 1. Podcast types and themes for you.......................18
   Part 2. Where to find them…...25
   Part 3. Where else to look… 31

Chapter 4 Reaching out to podcasts… to get a yes 34
   Part 1. Be specific..34
   Part 2. Remember about them!..39
   Part 3. Be prolific 41
   Part 4. Track your progress 43
   Part 5. Following up 46
   Part 6. Don't give up 48
   Bonus Part. Intro calls 49

Chapter 5 Preparing for your podcast appearance 51
   Part 1. Your key messages 51
   Part 2. Your Call To Action 57

Chapter 6 Showing up as your best self on the day..........59
    Part 1. Changing your state 59
    Part 2. Getting confident and relaxed.............................62

Chapter 7 Making the most of your podcast appearance after it airs **65**
    Part 1. Planning your social media content 65
    Part 2. Maximising the podcast content 68
    Part 3. Learning as you go…..71

Chapter 8 The End...73
    Summary and good luck..73

Worksheets..75

Template Emails..88

Important Links 92

ABOUT THE AUTHOR

LINDSAY REID has worked with some of the UK's best known brands and individuals throughout her media and PR career, spanning more than 20 years.

She has managed and delivered PR consultancy across a multitude of sectors including wellbeing, transport, entertainment, business, housing and others, for dozens of clients.

A growing part of her PR role is matching clients with the right podcasts to help them appear as a guest and grow their business - something that can be a true game changer for small businesses and entrepreneurs in growing their reach, audience, customer base and revenue.

This book pulls together everything Lindsay does on a day-to-day basis to find the right podcasts for her clients… and you can use all of it to find the right podcasts to for you and your business to make a guest appearance on.

Being a podcast guest can open new doors, boost your own confidence and help you reach a whole new audience.

Of course, not everyone can afford to hire a PR Consultant to do this work for them… but with this book, you can learn the simple skills and strategies needed to find the best podcasts for you and your business.

You'll learn…
- How to identify the best topics and content for you to talk about on podcasts
- How to search for and find the podcasts that are right for you and your business
- How to reach out to those podcasts to get a yes
- How to prepare for your podcast appearance and show up as your best self on the day
- How to make the most of your podcast appearance after it airs

So, let's get started…

CHAPTER 1
GETTING STARTED

Introduction

Welcome – you've already made a good choice by getting yourself a copy of this book so a huge welcome from me.

Just a quick note on my credentials… I've worked for more than 20 years in media and PR, as a journalist, as PR for a series of high-profile people and businesses, and also as a podcast host myself.

And my clients have appeared on many chart-topping podcasts including Mo Gawdat's Slow Mo podcast, Ellie McKay's On A Mission podcast, the Made By Mammas podcast, Matt Willis' On The Mend podcast, the Scummy Mummies podcast… and many more.

Plus, I'm a business owner - I run my own small business and I know all of the things that entails, including all of the joys of running your own business and all of the challenges. And there are many of both!

So, what's this all about? Well, put simply, it's about letting more people hear about you and your product or business… because the more people who hear about you, the more people will buy from you.

But we're not just talking about anyone and everyone - we want to focus on reaching the people you think are closest to your ideal customers, that do the kinds of things your ideal customers do and that want the same kinds of things that your ideal customers want.

Of course, in an ideal world you want to be actively invited on to podcasts… and have a stream of offers and podcast invites coming in for you. And if you become well known enough in your field, that will happen for sure.

But for now, we are building awareness around you and your business, and we are building your reputation. So, to do that we're reaching out and finding our own opportunities… being proactive (and prolific but I'll come on to that later!) is the key at this stage.

At the end of this book there are a series of worksheets relating to the activities we'll discuss in each chapter. I know the thought of doing activities feels a bit homeworky… but the reality is that unless we do the work, we don't get the best results we can.

So, I would urge, encourage and advise you to give these activities your best shot throughout the book.

You bought it afterall… so let's make sure you get the most out of it!

Why podcasts?

Now I would say this given my job, but I think podcasts are one of the best things to come out of the last decade, I really do. Why? Because they're so accessible, because almost anyone can start one and because there are so many genuine and important conversations that happen on podcasts thousands of times every day across the world that truly help the people listening to them.

Honestly, some of my most joyful moments in day-to-day life are when I'm out walking listening to a good podcast, or on a long drive with a great podcast for company. You canny beat it as we say in Scotland.

But on top of that, as a media channel, here's why I think they're great…

1) There are lots of them… so there are plenty of options available
2) They're usually pretty obvious in their niche/subject matter so it's a lot easier to find the ones that are best suited to you and your business… much easier that is than finding the right journalist at the right media outlet to cover your story.
3) Podcasts are a great chance for you to be heard authentically - it's your voice, your words and what you say is what people hear unlike other media channels where you might supply the information but other people convey it or write it the way they want to.
4) On top of that, podcasts usually allow you more time to say your piece, unlike media interviews or written articles where often only parts of your story can be used. Podcasts tend to be longer form so they give the listener/viewer more context around

your story and your business and not just one or the other.

5) Podcasts are personal and easy to consume, and people can consume them on the move, or while doing other things which - rightly or wrongly - is what a lot of people are looking for these days. Instead of sitting down for a few hours with a paper, or to read the online news, people are consuming podcasts while they walk, jog, drive, do the weekly shop, lie on their sunloungers on holiday, do their gardening or lots of other things.

And when I say they're personal, I mean, because they're often consumed while people are on the move, people listen to them through headphones which means it's quite a personal and intimate experience in some ways - your voice is going directly into their ears with no barriers in the way so the listener feels more like they know you because they feel like they've been so close to you.

So, all of the above are reasons why I love podcasts - there are just so many of them and there's literally a podcast for pretty much every niche known to humankind.

To be exact, as of February 2024, there are thought to be more than 4million podcasts in existence with over half a billion podcast listeners around the world So that's a hec of a lot of potential podcasts for you to appear on to grow your business.

So, let's get started…

CHAPTER 2
IT ALL STARTS WITH YOU

Part 1. Your goal

(Please see the Worksheets Section at the end of the book to complete the activities in this chapter – and future chapters)

OK, so you've got your business up and running and now it's time to bring podcasts into your marketing and media activities to help more people find out about what you offer - your product or services.

Whatever product, service, personal brand or story you want to share on a podcast, this book will help you do it.

And regardless of what you want to talk about… it's always best to start with your goal.

What are you trying to achieve through your podcast appearances? And why does that outcome matter?

Now it's easy at this point to quickly write down (on your worksheet at the back of the book) that you want to grow your business, make more sales, and earn more money because that will allow you to go on more holidays.

But we need to go deeper here for it to really resonate and mean something to you.

So… let's consider what you're trying to achieve through your podcast appearances, beyond having more people find out about your stuff.

What do you want these people to feel, think, know about you and your business?

What actions do you want them to take? Is there a first step to those actions that makes it easier for them i.e. a freebie they can access, social media they can find you on, or some kind of introduction that bridges the gap between them hearing about you and becoming a customer. Really think through the path you want these podcast listeners to take when they hear you speak.

What problem do you want the listeners to feel like you can solve for them? How are you going to do that? How are you going to show that you understand what their problem is, and articulate what your solution does and why they should choose it over other potential solutions?

Are you going to make them an offer maybe? Something that's too good to turn down.

Next, think about the why… maybe you do want to go on more holidays and that's ok! Of course it is. But a powerful way to tap into our why is to think about the feelings we want to create around the outcomes we're seeking.

So for me, when I think about why I want my businesses to succeed - I imagine the people I'm helping and how much easier things get for them because they found me. So, I imagine the business owner who has an amazing product but feels like it's the best kept secret ever - those are my people because I know I can help them share their story through what I teach.

And if I don't show up and tell them about my product? Well, they might stay stuck, or they might do endless other courses that don't give them the value they're paying for.

Who is your ideal customer? What do they need from you? And what will happen to them if you don't show up?

Also, really try to tap into the feelings you'll get when you achieve the outcome you want… will you feel proud? Joyful? Confident?

Imagine that moment when you feel those feelings… imagine telling your family or partner that you've achieved the thing you wanted to achieve… that you've helped the people you want to help. How do you feel in that moment?

Because attaching our aims to feelings and emotions is so powerful and a really strong driver to help us show up and do the work.

So now go ahead and complete Worksheet 1 before you move on to the next part.

Part 2. Finding Your Voice

I've heard a lot of people saying recently, if you can't think of things to say about your business each day then maybe you're in the wrong business - and I get where they're coming from - BUT as much as we might know inside our heads all about our business and what we do, it's one thing knowing that and it's another thing talking about it and really expressing the things we want to express about our business.

And that, in my experiences, is THE big reason why business owners avoid podcasts - because they don't feel confident enough to speak in public about their business. They become overwhelmed by the thought of it, convince themselves they'll make a fool of themselves and avoid it completely. If this is you, you're definitely not alone!

So, how do we get out of that mindset and find our voice…

Well first, let's remember something super important - NOBODY knows your business as well as you do. And that's a fact. DO NOT FORGET THAT! (Sorry for shouting but it's important!).

When you speak about your business, nobody except you knows what you want to say… and on the flip side, if you miss bits out, nobody except you is even aware of it. So, if you look at it like that, the pressure is completely off.

So hopefully that's our number one panic removed - if you're worried about forgetting what you want to say or making a fool of yourself it's just not going to happen.

A lot about finding your voice comes in the preparation. And here's the best news. With podcasts you tend to have plenty time to prepare. Almost never are they sprung on you with minutes to spare so you're never going to be put on the spot without even having had a chance to think about what you want to say. That pretty much never happens.

Yet when we think about podcasts that's the pressure situation, we seem to imagine… and yes that would be slightly intimidating for anyone. But the reality is that's not what it's like at all. The podcast tends to be booked in ahead of time giving you a chance to think about what you want to say and what you want people to hear about your business.

OK, so big panic element number 2 has now been removed - you will not be dropped in at the deep end.

So, now let's get a bit more focused on the six questions in the next worksheet… to help you find your voice and your messaging.

1) What about me makes me the best person to talk about my business?
2) What's the first thing I always tell people about my business… and why?
3) If I only had one sentence to describe my business, what would I say?
4) What makes my business different from others and a bit more extra special? (Name 3 things at least)
5) In what ways am I good at what I do? (Name 3 things at ways!)
6) What are my main achievements in business (and /or life) over the past 5 years? (Write at least 10 things!)

By answering these questions, we're starting to form some great generic messages that we want people to hear about us and our business (don't worry, we'll work on more specific ones later) and we're also - more importantly - reminding ourselves what's so flippin' amazing about us and our businesses, something we probably never do!

And I know you're amazing and committed and hard working - or you wouldn't be here doing this course.

Hopefully you know that as well, but for some of us that info tends to live buried away deep down, so this is a great chance to bring it back to the surface.

Afterall, if you want to promote your business you have to remind yourself why it matters, what's so good about it, what are the most important things you want people to know about it and why you do what you do - and conveniently, we're moving on to that in the next part.

Head over to WORKSHEET 2 and complete those questions before moving on to the next section.

Part 3. Passion for what you do

Now, in order to make a real impact during a podcast, the human side of your business has to shine through and the people listening need to get a sense of not only who you are and what you do, but why you do it and why you enjoy it.

Nobody wants to hear podcasts with business owners reeling off facts and figures and achievements and targets… they want to hear about the person or people involved, the human stories and the vulnerabilities, struggles and even humour along the way.

Never forget that although you're showing up on podcasts as a business owner, you're a human being first and foremost and it's that human side of us that connects with other humans.

So, we covered your why in a previous lesson as more of a reminder as to why you're even doing all this in the first place… and to keep your goals front of mind.

This lesson is more about bringing out your passion and enjoyment for what you do, so that it shines through in any podcast.

Don't be fooled into thinking we want embellished stories and dramatised scenarios - it's not about being as entertaining as possible. This is about you being the real you but in a way that incorporates a bit more storytelling perhaps and invokes some relatable human emotions.

And here's a great HOT TIP in this lesson - when you're describing something that happened or a situation you found yourself in, there's one simple thing you can do that will 10 times the impact of your story - and that thing is including how you felt at the time of the thing you're describing.

For example, if I tell a story about the build up to the first big event that I organised, I might talk about the challenges of dealing with suppliers, the amount of emails I sent out, the amount of time I had to dedicate to it and the things that went well and went wrong along the way.

But if I talk about all of those things AND say that during all of that I felt terrified, stressed, exhilarated, panicked and woke up in a cold sweat feeling anxious most nights… that makes it a lot more powerful… and relatable.

Don't wait for the podcast host to ask you how you felt… include it in your stories and recollections from the start.

Another reason for approaching it this way is that reminding yourself of the rollercoaster of feelings you've experienced through running your business is a great way to tap into your passion for what you do.

And this is the main point of this lesson - we want our passion as business owners to shine through in podcasts, not because we're directly telling listeners that we're passionate about our business, but because our passion and enjoyment for what we do is weaved into the stories that we tell and the way we talk about our business.

To help with this, we need to remind ourselves - because it's easy to forget in the day-to-day slog - what we love about what we do.

*So now use **WORKSHEET 3***
to answer these questions below…
and then move on to the next chapter.

What 5 things do I love most about my business?

If my business didn't exist what would life look like for the people who have benefited from it?

Who is my happiest client, why were they helped by my business and how did they feel?

When have I felt happiest in my business journey? Why was that?

In what ways does my business improve my life? (Name at least 5).

CHAPTER 3
FINDING THE PERFECT PODCASTS FOR YOUR BUSINESS...

Part 1. Podcast types and themes for you

Right, now that we've looked inside ourselves and pulled out lots of great messaging about our business, it's time to start looking externally... and finding all those podcasts for us to potentially be a guest on.

So, in this chapter, there are three parts covering the different types and themes of podcasts that will work for you... along with lots of practical advice and tips on where to find podcast opportunities for yourself.

Let's start with the kinds of podcast you might want to appear on… and you might think well, that's easy, just the ones in my niche… but wait. Because something a lot of people do is narrow their vision way too much when it comes to the kinds of podcasts they might approach or think about appearing on.

What we have to do here is keep an open mind, do some creative thinking and then watch as our list of opportunities grows and grows.

So, this is where we start small… and then think bigger until we have a long list of possibilities.

Obviously with podcasts there are some broad parameters that are quite obvious i.e. if you're English speaking and you don't speak any other languages then you're not going to be approaching French, or Spanish speaking podcasts - let's just stick to the English-speaking podcasts in that case.

Or if you have a product that's only available to buy in the UK, or to be shipped within the UK, then let's not look for Australian and US podcasts right now. However, with that I'm talking about a physical product. Say for example, you're an online coach, and can accept any English-speaking clients, then these countries could provide some great options for you.

So, think about your business - where do you sell? Where are your current customers based? And let's go with that as a baseline.

Now you'll probably know right away what your niche is… i.e. what space do you operate in? Is it life coaching? Selling cakes? Running a gym? Running a marketing agency? Selling jewellery? Running a cafe? What would you class as your 'space'?

So that's great - but that's just one option for you. Yes, it's possibly the strongest option but there will be other strong options out there too if we get creative.

Here's an example. If I run woodwork lessons, I'd probably say my niche for podcasts would be woodwork… makes sense.

But there are a whole other host of wider niches that I could also tap into. For example…

- Running a small business
- Learning a new skill
- Taking up a hobby
- Mental health
- Mindfulness
- Confidence and self-development

See what I mean? All of the above audiences might also be interested in hearing about what you do and, more importantly, buying your product.

And then there might also be an aspect of you or your back story that relates to other niches again… for example…

    Being a certain age i.e. under 30 / midlife / over 50
    Being alcohol-free
    Overcoming adversity
    Parenting / Parenting teenagers / Parenting toddlers
    Grief / loss
    Body image
    Mental Health
    Community
    Friendship
    Bankruptcy / money successes
    Being part of the LGBTQ+ community
    Geography of where you live

These are just a few examples and there are tonnes more… again these can all be relevant to your potential audience. Even though they're more personal subjects, they allow people to relate to you as a person and to understand why you do what you do.

So, from one obvious niche, we can expand out (and this took me literally seconds to get about 12 different options of themes that this woodwork teacher could tap into. If I spent longer on it, I'd absolutely come up with more.

Now, when it comes to the more personal themes, obviously we can only choose to talk about them if we're comfortable doing so. There is absolutely no NEED for you to do that if you don't want to, and that's really important.

I've worked with tonnes of business owners who will happily chat away about all aspects of their life and that's great. And I've worked with lots who would rather keep some of the more personal things about their story private… and that's great too.

You have to do whatever works for you… or it doesn't work at all.

So, here's the good part where you can get creative and start thinking about all of the potential themes and niches you can tap into when it comes to podcasts… once you get going, I can almost guarantee you'll start to get excited about the possibilities.

And please remember this… when it comes to the wider themes that seem further away from your central niche, you don't have to be an expert in the subject you're talking about, or have qualifications or certificates. You are an expert in your own experience of whatever you're talking about so you are perfectly entitled and qualified to talk about it.

Too often we think we're not 'qualified' to talk about something that we have lived experience of. And let me tell you - if we have lived experience of it, we're ALWAYS qualified to talk about it.

So now head to the LINKS section at the end of the book and either log into the Podcast Matching Worksheet via link provided or create your own spreadsheet based on the image provided.

Firstly, write down your CENTRAL NICHE - this will be your main subject matter (1 or 2 things here max) i.e. around what your business sells or delivers or the industry you're in.

Then next section is around your WIDER THEMES… thinking more widely list the other elements of life and business that your work touches. To help with this, think of some of the benefits that people get from using your product… i.e. confidence, skills… and also think of your skill set as a business owner - what can you talk about in relation to being a business owner? Entrepreneurship? Marketing? Product creation? Building communities? Building strong working relationships?

List down as many as you can possibly think of.

And then, for the third and final section, we're looking at PERSONAL THEMES - so these are things you've experienced in your life - which ideally have contributed in some way to what you're doing now - that you're comfortable to talk about.

So, ask yourself, what adversity have you been through? Money worries? Mental health struggles? Becoming a parent? Overhauling your fitness?

Or what are the main elements of your life? Fitness? Hiking? Cooking? Music?

List all of these things down too.

And so at the end of this activity we should have at least 15-20 options of podcast subjects and themes that are in some way relevant to us, that we now want to explore.

Part 2. Where to find them....

So, we're now at the point where you should have a nice long list of potential niches and themes of podcasts that you want to tap into.

Now we have to find the right ones for your business… and I'm not going to lie… this is fairly simple but it's not easy and it does take effort.

BUT we know it's going to be worth it right, and we know from the first module WHY we are doing this, so it's that why that helps us show up for the work that's involved in this part.

And it's that WHY that we need to keep coming back to if and when it feels like a slog.

My HOT tip here is small steps consistently is what achieves results.

You might want to do a good stint of this research to get you started but after that I strongly suggest a little bit each day is more effective than trying to chunk it all into a few long sessions. If you commit to 20mins or half an hour a day I guarantee within a couple of weeks you'll have a decent list of potential podcasts to start reaching out to.

If you try to do too much at once it'll feel too much like a chore - and then the next time you know you have to do it, you'll put it off for as long as possible. And we don't want that.

So, we have our list of themes so now we simply start searching… and we search in all different ways until we find what we're looking for.

To be honest, I know this is a book but the easiest way for me to show you how I do this process from start to finish is through two videos I have made showing it from start to finish.

Video 1

This shows how I use Apple podcasts to search and find suitable podcasts for my clients, using the key words and search terms that I can think of for their specific areas of interest and things they can talk about… from a list just like the one you have created in the previous chapter.

I simply type the search terms into Apple podcasts app (I use it on my mac but you could do it on your phone too, and you could also use other podcast platforms like Spotify etc. as well) and then go through all of the results that it throws up checking whether each podcast might be a good fit for my client.

The key things I consider are:

- When the last episode of the podcast aired (if longer than two months previous, I would probably leave it for now, or check back at a later date)

- How many episodes they have released (the more the better as it shows they're well established

- How many reviews they have (again, the more the better especially if they're good ones!!)

- Whether they're based in the UK, US or elsewhere and whether that will work for my client

- Whether the things they seem to chat about and their style of chat would suit my client and their style of chat/their topics and content - I'd usually do this by listening to the podcast for a few episodes, or part of episodes, to get a feel for what they do and how they do it.

- Again, none of what I'm doing is rocket science - far from it - but I just thought it might help when you come to do this as a) it shows how simple it is and b) I know it works because I do it every day with great results.

To see what I'm talking about in video format go to the LINKS section at the end of the book and access the video showing this by using the link provided for Video 1.

Video 2

Moving on to the next stage of the process, it's all about tracking down those all important contact details for the podcasts we want to get in touch with.

Now some are wonderfully helpful and include a contact email address in the podcast notes (the podcast description) - this is like the promised land when you're doing what we're doing!! Happy days indeed!

Some also provide a website in the podcast description, and sometimes you can get other contact details from there.

But most podcasts don't provide ready-made contact details and that's when we have to get out sleuthing and research skills out and just get searching – step forward Google (or whatever your preferred search engine!)!

Often it takes some online research around the podcast, or around the hosts, to be able to find contact details for them, sometimes in the following ways.

The host may have a website of their own… often you'll find contact details on there.

If not, they're more than likely to have a social media presence - usually we can find them on Instagram or Facebook (they're the main ones I use) as well as LinkedIn which I use occasionally. Or of course there are others like TikTok and X (Twitter) which to be honest I don't use much, but they might be your preferred platforms so again it's about finding what works for you.

HOT TIP – if using Instagram like I do a lot, always check out someone's profile on your phone as more often than not the 'Email 'option within their profile on shows up on the mobile phone version of Instagram and not on the computer version. So you might look on the computer version and think there's no email address provided - only the option to message that person - but then if you look on your phone, you might well have an 'Email 'or 'Contact 'button that wasn't showing on your computer version.

Sometimes the host has a different business and you can track them down that way by email.

And then sometimes it's super tricky to find an email address for someone, in which case you might have to resort to messaging them on social media which is my least preferred option as, in my experience, a lot of people a) don't read their DMs and b) you have to do a bit of work to shorten your outreach message to fit in with the character guidelines of the platform.

Another thing to note is that sometimes podcasts are produced by a third party, either a person or a production company, and if you're struggling to find contact details for the podcast or host, it can be well worth looking up the producer or production company and making an approach through them (not least because they might also work on other podcasts that they might think will be a good fit for you).

Not long ago, I reached out to a production company on behalf of a client and they came back and offered him a guest slot on a totally different - but excellent – podcast than the one I had initially had in mind!

So the moral of this part is, get curious, become investigative and treat it as a bit of a challenge or a game to see what ways you can use to find a suitable contact detail for the podcasts you'd like to reach out to.

Some will be easier to find than others but that's all part of the fun!

Access all of this in video format go to the LINKS section at the end of the book and access the video showing this by using the link provided for Video 2.

Part 3. Where else to look...

Now we're going to talk about other ways to find podcasts that don't involve lots of online searching.

Here are some of the main ways I hear about new podcasts on top of my own searches - and that's the key here. These are things I do IN ADDITION to my online searches... not instead of them.

1) Social media - I can't tell you the amount of screen grabs I have saved on my phone that I've taken from Instagram or Facebook (they're the main channels I use) whenever I see someone, I follow has appeared on a podcast I haven't heard of, or maybe someone has started a new podcast that they're posting about. So be vigilant on your social media... look out for people talking about podcasts they've been on or promoting their own podcasts and instead of just scrolling past it, screengrab it and add it to your list of podcasts to look into.

2) Your competitors... to take the above point a step further you can always actively keep an eye on what your competitors are doing, if they've been on any podcasts which ones? Think about what can you talk about that differs from them? What can you zero in on that seems to have worked for them?

3) Facebook groups - there are Facebook groups specifically designed for podcast hosts and podcast guests to find each other. These can work well sometimes… although often there's a lot of people in these groups and therefore a lot of people responding all at one time to shout-outs by podcast hosts so it can be tricky to be noticed among the crowd.

If you do respond to these groups you have to be able to sell yourself and your story succinctly and interestingly in order to get noticed - we'll cover this in the next chapter.

Also, think about any other Facebook groups you might be in - maybe they're business-related or based on a specific theme - you can even do a search of the word 'podcast(s)' in these groups and see what pops up. You might find that people have asked about podcasts before and been given info that's also helpful to you. You just never know!

4) Meet-ups and events - believe it or not sometimes the old face to face way of meeting new people can still be one of the most effective. There are networking events all over the place these days and more than likely even at generic business networking events there will be a few people who have their own podcasts and know others than do. Go along and get chatting to people - it really works.

Online networking is still a great option too if there aren't many face to face opportunities near you.

And with meet-up sites there are podcast specific events and groups in most towns and cities these days so again just seek them out online and then maybe get along to a few and give them a go.

5) Listen to podcasts!! I know it sounds obvious but often podcast hosts and guests mention other podcast hosts and guests so try to listen to a variety of podcasts and you never know, you might just pick up some nice tips on new podcasts, podcasts with new series starting and people's favourites that you might not already have heard of.

Basically, you kind of end up training your brain to notice all things podcast related. That's what I do - every time I spot something or hear something about a new podcast I treat it like a new lead and look into it… some work out, some don't but it's amazing the number of times that something positive can come of it either directly or indirectly.

Try to approach it with curiousity and you'll enjoy this part of the process a whole lot more!

CHAPTER 4
REACHING OUT TO PODCASTS...
TO GET A YES

Part 1. Be specific

Right, we've got to the point where we know what we want to talk about and we've pulled together a list of podcasts that we think will be a good fit for us.

Now, we need to reach out to those podcasts and hopefully encourage them to allow us on as guests!

So for this, we need to get specific - about ourselves and about our potential podcasts.

Now head to WORKSHEET 4 at the end of the book

The aim here is to get really clear on what we are bringing to the table… and good way to do this is to use stats. Now you might not think you have many impressive stats but don't panic - you probably have more than you think.

So in the worksheet note down first any of the below stats you can complete (preview below) and then come back to the rest of this section once you've done that.

xx years' experience in your chosen field/subject you want to talk about

xx clients / customers supported (round to dozens, hundreds, thousands)

xx followers on social media (again round up so if 2,350 followers say almost 2,500)

Previous podcasts you might have been on that supports your case to appear on the one you're reaching out to

Any high profile people you've worked with that strengthens your case as a guest

Any awards you've won (then you can describe your business as award-winning which is powerful)

Any media coverage you've had in the past (i.e. as featured in / on

Anything else you feel strengthens your case to be on their show and demonstrates the value you'd bring to their audience.

Great, now you've got a good bank of info about yourself/your business and this can be used pretty much for most podcasts you're going to approach.

But here's the second part of this lesson in being specific. It's super important to be specific in your approach to the podcast and what I mean by that is you need tailor your approach to them in particular and show that you've got a good understanding of what they're looking for.

And my first HOT tip here is - LISTEN to the podcast you want to reach out to. It sounds like daft advice but it's so easy when you're searching to find a podcast you think is a good potential, and then get excited and reach out to them with a quick generic email or message.

The reality is it's so much more impactful to spend some time listening to a few of their episodes, getting a feel for their approach, their tone and their content, and then writing something that is specific to them, that shows you get where they're coming from and positions you as a much better fit than a generic email would.

Believe me, I've done the shortcut - not many times to be honest because I realised quickly it just doesn't work - so make sure before you do any kind of outreach to a podcast, you listen to a few episodes first to familiarise yourself with it.

That way you can tap into the kinds of themes that you know they enjoy talking about… or you can side with an opinion that you might have heard a host share… showing that you're a good fit.

There's more to it than just copying and pasting the same email to a load of podcasts - and paying extra attention to this will glean better results.

Of course, there are parts of our approach that we can use again and again - we don't have to completely re-write the whole email each time - but we do have to give it some thought and tailor it as much as we can to that particular podcast… if we want to give ourselves the best chance of getting a yes that is.

At the end of the book you'll find a template email that you can use as an example when writing yours, or simply tailor to make it relevant to you and your business.

Visit the TEMPLATES section at the end of the book to access your outreach email template.

Part 2. Remember about them!

This part is all about the biggest mistake that people make when reaching out to podcasts - they make it all about themselves… and they forget to consider what the podcast host wants to get out of it.

We have to remember why people host podcasts - most of the time it's not just for fun, even if they enjoy it. No, most of the time there's a reason behind it - they want to reach more people and sell them their product, just you do.

So if they're showing up regularly and giving their time to this podcast then they want to feel like it's worth and therefore they want to bring guests that are going to help them achieve their objective.

Usually podcast hosts are looking for a few main things.

1) Someone who can bring them an audience - a new audience that they can then add to their own audience. So if you have a decent following on social media, potentially as many or more followers than them, then they probably feel like they'll get a benefit out of that.

But side note - we all know that follower numbers don't actually mean a huge amount so this is definitely not the be all and end all and I am absolutely not saying only reach out to podcasts that have the same kind of follower number as you. What I am saying is if you have the same or more than them, then it might be worth mentioning that in your pitch.

There are other ways to demonstrate your audience too - for example if you have an email list you can tell them you'll share the episode with your 1,000-strong email list, or whatever it might be.

2) They want a compelling story - they want you to bring something interesting and entertaining to their listeners, whether that's you sharing an experience you've had, or a big life-changing moment you experienced, or something very cool or quirky about you or your business, they want to feel like they're bringing interesting, fresh content to their listeners so that's what you want to tell them that you'll provide.

3) They want value for their listeners - what can you teach their audience? How will they benefit from hearing you? What will you contribute to their lives if they listen? All good podcast hosts want to provide value to their audience and for people to feel like they're learning and growing when they listen.

4) And I guess the other thing podcast hosts want is, as I mentioned earlier, to feel like they're doing a good job so, without being disingenuous about it of course,

we want to help remind them that their podcast is helping people.

One of the best ways to sell anything to anyone is to really show them the benefits they'll get from saying yes and it's no different here - yes, we want to share information to show we're worthy guests but we also want to make clear what we bring to the table and why that's positive for their podcast.

Part 3. Be prolific

This part is called Be Prolific - simply because that's what you've got to be when doing your outreach to podcasts.

When I work with clients, I keep a tracking list of all of the outreach I've done for them… and I can tell you it takes a decent amount of reaching out to get the results you want.

Most of my client lists have at least 80-100 outreach on them within a couple of months, and way more again beyond that, because I know that in order to get enough yesses and the kind of yesses they want, I have to reach out to a lot of people.

It's a numbers game - like on your social media. If you know only a small % of your social media audience will buy from you, then you have to try and grow your audience so that the small % translates into more people.

And if you know that only a small(ish) % of the podcasts you reach out to will say yes (certainly initially), then you have to reach out to as many as possible to try and grow that number.

And the advice I gave with the research applies here too - build this up in a way that allows you to do your outreach consistently so that you can keep it up over a long period of time.

Even if you commit to doing 20-30mins a day of outreach, or to sending out 2-3 outreach emails a day, over time those numbers will build up.

So look at it like a long-term goal - yes, you want some nice quick wins and hopefully you'll get some of those, but what we want is to keep going, consistently adding to the list of people we're reaching out to, and thereby increasing our chances of getting the outcome we want.

Part 4. Track your progress

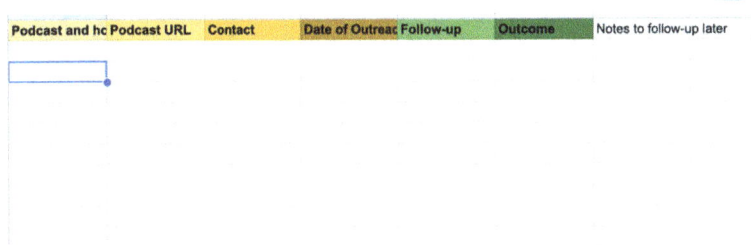

OK, once we find a podcast that we think works for us, we can add it into the Podcast Tracking Worksheet and note down when and how we did our outreach to them, just to keep us right.

This is exactly how I track my outreach when reaching out to podcasts on behalf of my clients.

Hopefully it will help you do the same for your outreach so you can always check back to who you've approached and when… even though you think it'll be simple enough to remember that kind of thing, believe me, when you're busy with other things as well, it's amazing how quickly you forget.

So having it all tracked just means you don't have to search through hundreds of emails to check something.

I do this in two simple stages.

Stage 1

Basically, as you'll see when you visit the Podcast Tracking Worksheet, when I find a suitable podcast I write the name of it and the name of the host in Column A of the worksheet.

Then in Column B I add the link to the podcast so I can re-visit it any time if there's something I want to check, without having to search all over again for it.

And in Column C I add in the contact details I've found for the podcast - these are the details I will use for my outreach.

Stage 2

At this point I'm ready to do my outreach - sometimes I might do outreach as soon as I find a podcast or sometimes I might pull together a list of podcasts first and then do a few separate outreach sessions to work my way through the list - it's just about finding what works for you.

Either way, once I've done my outreach, I go back to the Podcast Tracking Worksheet and in Column D I note down the date of my outreach.

Then in Column E, I will add in the date that I send a follow-up to that podcast (if relevant) and in Column

F I will write in the outcome of my outreach. This could be something like:

Yes, recording date set/recording date TBC

Yes, but full guestlist right now - follow-up later in the year

Thanks, but no thanks

No reply

And there's space in Column G to note anything down that you want to remember in particular about that podcast.

We always think we'll remember things but, believe me, when you do a lot of these it's amazing how quickly you forget or get mixed up between podcasts.

So, that's how I use the Podcast Tracking Worksheet - simply to keep myself right about what I've done, who I've reached out to and when and any actions needed for the future.

I told you it was simple! I wasn't blessed with a load of technical skills so basics are best for me all the way!

To see what I'm talking about, or start your own tracking worksheet, head to the LINKS section at the end of the book and either log into the Podcast

Tracking Worksheet via the link provided or create your own spreadsheet based on the image provided.

Part 5. Following up

A lot of successful sales people - and coaches I've had myself in the past - talk about the fortune being in the follow-up.

Now, in my experience, something similar could be said of podcast outreach - maybe not the fortune exactly but there definitely lies success in the follow-up.

So, what do I mean by follow-up? Well, if you've sent an outreach email to a podcast host and had no reply, then it would be time to do a follow-up email.

When is good to do a follow-up? I would generally say a few weeks after your original email, possibly 2-3 weeks.

Why follow-up? Well quite simply because people are busy and people are forgetful. Yes, I'm a big believer that a lot of people who are going to reply with a yes to this kind of thing will do it right away… BUT I also know from experience that just because someone doesn't reply with a yes right away doesn't mean they're not interested.

In my experience, when you follow-up you can get people apologising that they missed the first email and saying yes, saying they've been busy and forgot to reply and saying yes, or simply giving you useful info like they're taking a break from the podcast, or maybe they're booked up with guests and ask you to give them a shout again in a couple of months.

I've had all of these responses to follow-ups I've sent out in the past.

So please remember you're entitled to follow up - it's not harassment! If they haven't replied to your first approach to say no, then you're entitled to check in with them a second time.

Personally, if I didn't hear from them again on the second approach, I would leave it.

But remember you're offering them something of value - you! So there's no need to feel bad about chasing up - in fact you're doing them a disservice if you don't as they might have just missed your first email and missed the chance to have you as a great guest if you don't send the follow-up.

Visit the TEMPLATES page at the end of the book to access your follow-up email template.

Part 6. Don't give up

This is your reminder not to give up.

Please believe me when I say if you keep going at this for long enough, reaching out to enough people and refining an improving your approach, then you will get some results.

But it can be disheartening when maybe you go a couple of weeks without getting a yes, or even a reply.

I know that feeling… but in my experience, the only thing to do in that situation is keep going.

And over time, you'll learn that the yesses you do get are enough to keep you going and to keep believing even if there are more nos!

This is like anything new that you're starting… you have to look long-term, build it into your routine and keep going with a consistent approach to get the best results.

A huge part of being successful at anything is showing up and doing the work when you can't see the results. And that applies here.

So keep plugging away and don't give up. You'll be glad you did.

Bonus Part. Intro calls

Sometimes when you reach out to a podcast host, they'll be interested but because you're essentially a stranger to them, they might prefer to have an intro call with you first.

This can be a good idea for them because a) they get a sense of your energy and how you come across, and b) they can get a sense of the main themes they want to talk about during the recording.

To be honest, I am sometimes surprised that more podcast hosts don't do intro calls before they book guests they don't know… but then it can be time consuming. I do know a couple of podcast hosts who insist on intro calls before they confirm the booking.

So don't be surprised (or disappointed) if people ask for an intro call - it's a great sign as it means they're interested in you. And it's also a good chance for you to get a sense of what makes them tick and what might make a great conversation between the two of you.

The main thing to remember about an intro call is not to treat it like a test. Just think of it as having a conversation with someone new.

Don't try and sell yourself too much - but be prepared to share succinctly what you do and why you do it.

Have one or two wee stories up your sleeve to demonstrate things you're talking about.

And ask the host about them! Talk about something you've enjoyed about their podcast. Be interested in the journey they're on - try not to make it all about you.

Just think of it like a relaxed chat - if anything, intro calls make it more relaxing to do the podcast recording because you're already familiar with the podcast host, the way they ask questions and the subjects you've spoken about.

So, intro calls are good - say yes if you get asked to do one and then just show up with a sense of positive energy and warmth to make a good impression, just as you would want to do meeting anyone for the first time.

CHAPTER 5
PREPARING FOR YOUR PODCAST APPEARANCE

Part 1. Your key messages

Now, to recap quickly - up until this point we've identified our key messages, figured out the podcasts we think are a good fit for us and our business, and we've reached out to a nice big list of podcasts to offer our services a guest.

Now, we're going to assume that some of those podcasts have said yes - yay!!

But then, like all good humans, when someone says yes to us doing something that maybe makes us a bit nervous, we might get excited (quite rightly because it means our outreach has worked!) but then we probably immediately start to panic about actually doing the thing, which in this case is appearing on the podcast.

So, we're pleased that our work up until now has got us a result, but now we're scared of the next part!

So now let's look at preparing for our podcast appearance to help us make the most of it.

Firstly, let's not be scared - some nerves are normal and to be honest they show us that we care about doing a good job on this podcast, which is great. So, nerves are fine, maybe even good.

And remember, we WANT to do this for the good of our business.

And also remember we are QUALIFIED AND ABLE to talk about the things we told them we'd talk about.

No imposter syndrome is allowed around here!

If you've been accepted on to a podcast, then clearly the podcast host has every confidence that you can being some interesting chat and content to the table… that's all the evidence you need to show up. If they can believe in you, and they might not ever have met you before, then you can believe in you too.

Feeling scared or nervous is NOT a sign that we shouldn't do this… it's a normal part of stepping out of our comfort zone.

To help us feel more confident, we're going to make sure we're 100% prepared in what we want to say. I cannot stress enough how important preparation is. I've done it myself where I've tried to wing it and it's been stressful and uncomfortable and not worked out how I wanted it to. And I've worked with PR clients in the past who - regardless of how many times I told them to go over their script or look at interview questions in advance - left it all to the last minute and didn't make the most of the opportunity as a result.

We don't want to obsess over this but we do want to feel nicely prepared.

To do this, I would write down two sets of notes…

The first set is a list of questions you think you'll be asked… write down as many as you can think of. What would you ask you if you were hosting a podcast?

And then make sure you have an answer for these questions - not a word for word answer, but just a broad idea of what you'll say if you're asked that question.

If there's anything tricky or controversial you think you will be asked then it's even more important to have an answer prepared.

For example, if you're a menopause coach and a new regulation has come out about how workplaces treat women during menopause (as happened not too long ago) there's a fair chance you'll get asked about that so make sure you have an answer prepared.

The second set of notes will be around the messages you absolutely MUST get across during this podcast chat - what 2 or 3 things do you want the listeners to know about you and your business by the end of the episode?

And I say 2 or 3 things because it's overwhelming if we have too many - and we're talking absolute non-negotiables here that you must not leave the podcast recording without saying! These are not just nice to haves - these are things you think the audience absolutely must learn about you and your business. It might even just be one or two… write them down and make sure you know them off by heart.

Finally for this lesson, think about dopping in some social proof that strengthens your case as an expert on this. When I say social proof, I basically mean say things that show that other people are using your products and benefitting from them.

For example, if you're a careers coach you could drop into the conversation, that you were just chatting to a former client who has started a new job at twice the salary she was on before… thereby showing that people (i.e. this former client) buy your stuff, and it benefits them.

Or you could give an example of when you used your own product - i.e. if you had a recipe or cooking app you might tell how you had to cook for 12 people last night so you picked one of your recipe cards out and just went with that, and it was a great success.

You see the kind of thing I mean?

Try to think of one or two examples of this nature, or short stories you can tell about clients or former clients which really show you and your business at your best and demonstrate you delivering the kind of results that you know a lot of the listeners will want too.

So the main takeaway from this part is don't panic, don't talk yourself out of it, and do your preparation!

And tell yourself over and over again the reasons why you're showing up in this way and the reasons why you know you can do this!

***Visit Worksheet 5 at the end of the book
and complete the questions before
moving on to the next part***

Part 2. Your Call To Action

Lastly in this chapter, we need to look at your CTA, or your Call To Action.

Remember the objective of going on the podcast is a) for more people to find out about your stuff and b) for them to learn how to engage with your stuff.

So, what's your call to action for people who hear the podcast? What are you asking them to do? What step are you inviting them to take after they've listened to you?

Occasionally people will offer a discounted rate on something on podcasts - through a promo code given to the podcast host perhaps - and you can do that of course, if you think it'll work well for your business.

But I think it's important to remember that the vast majority of the people listening will never have heard of you or your business before that episode - therefore we should probably assume that the likelihood that they're going to buy from you straight away is pretty low.

So, I would suggest you use the podcast instead to pull them into your own channels where they can find out more about what you do, learn about you and become a customer over time.

So perhaps point them to your social media channels, or perhaps even your own podcast if you have one, or your website.

And think of the podcast as a way of getting more people into your container who are interested and will hopefully become customers.

OR, another great option is to offer a freebie so you might say I've actually got a free cheat sheet for generating social media content on my website - all you have to do is visit the website and you can download it completely free.

Or another example might be - check out my Instagram page for lots of free advice on how to become a more calm parent.

Or visit my YouTube where I've got dozens of videos showing you my favourite cup cake recipes. These are examples but you get the idea.

Just remember, this is about baby steps - yes, we want to entice them gently into your world but we don't want to appear salesy or pushy, we just want them to come and join our journey.

CHAPTER 6
SHOWING UP AS YOUR BEST SELF ON THE DAY

Part 1. Changing your state

Well, this is getting exciting - we've done all of the prep and now the day of our podcast recording has arrived!

If you're new to podcasts or you always get a bit anxious having to talk in public - then this can be a bit of a nervewracking day. BUT it should be a lot less nervewracking now that we've done so much preparation throughout the previous chapters.

So, in actual fact, let's choose to get excited about this podcast recording! This is our opportunity - the one we've been working towards - to get our message across to potential new customers about our business.

Yee haa!

So whether the podcast is being recorded in person or via a video call, we need your energy to be positive and high vibes - as that's what you want people to feel from you when they hear you talk.

Therefore it's important that we get into a positive and energised state before the podcast. Think of the things that help you feel positive and energised - it could be getting some fresh air, listening to an upbeat song, doing some cleaning, speaking to someone who helps you feel good - think of what works for you.

For me, I usually find that the quickest and easiest way to change my state is to move my body. So I might go a walk, or even do some star jumps or something, to raise my heart rate and feel more energised.

Think of it as a warm up - it might sound strange - but why do you think athletes and sports teams spend so much time warming up before their big moment/game or match - because it helps them show up ready to do their best.

So, it's your responsibility to show up to that podcast recording as your best self, in an optimal state, so think about how you're going to do that and have a plan in place for the day to help you achieve that.

Part 2. Getting confident and relaxed

As well as being in a positive state, we really want to feel confident and relaxed when we go into the podcast.

So again, have your notes all ready of anything you feel you need a reminder of i.e. your key non-negotiable things you must not forget to tell people. Obviously if it's a podcast that's recorded in person it's better not to be looking at notes etc. so try to remember your top top key messages by heart if you can, but if it's a video call there's no harm in having a few notes in front of you - as long as you're not looking down at them all of the time - make eye contact with the host remember, don't look at notes the whole time!

When I say notes, I literally mean those 2-3 bullet points that you absolutely must remember to get across to the audience. So not pages and pages of everything you want to say… that won't work.

But have them if they help you feel more relaxed and confident.

Sometimes podcasts follow the same format every week - same questions, same order etc. so then you will know in advance exactly what you're going to be asked.

Sometimes podcast hosts offer to send their suggested questions to you and in my view it's useful to say yes to if they do ask.

If you're really worried and nervous - or maybe it's your first ever podcast - you could ask them to send questions over in advance but to be honest I would suggest against this because a) it creates more work for the podcast host which let's face it, nobody wants.

And b) I have every confidence - and so should you - that you can answer any adhoc questions about your business. Why? Because it's YOUR business, and because you know your stuff.

Don't forget that!!

So you should be feeling pretty confident because you've done your prep, you have your notes if you need them, and you believe in your own knowledge and ability to talk about what you are there to talk about.

Now you just need to make sure you're nice and relaxed so your thoughts can flow and you're nice and tuned into what you're being asked and what you're saying.

So, how do you relax? Is it deep breathing, meditating, journaling, going for a walk, sitting in the back garden for a few minutes?

Whatever it is, do it… it will absolutely help combat any last-minute nerves and 100% you'll feel the benefit when the time comes.

CHAPTER 7
MAKING THE MOST OF YOUR PODCAST APPEARANCE AFTER IT AIRS

Part 1. Planning your social media content

OK, so you've recorded the podcast - yay! But that's only one part of the job done - now it's super important that you get the most out of that podcast appearance by using it in as many ways as you can throughout your own channels.

Usually (not always, bus usually) there's at least a week or so (often more) between recording a podcast and the episode being aired - so you have time to think about and prep some social media around it. Of course, you can ask the podcast host when it's likely to be out, or to give you a shout.

At the very bare minimum you want to be sharing the posts the hosts publish on their channels so I know it sounds simple and a bit daft, but the first thing to do is make sure they have the correct social media handles for you… so they tag the right account when sharing the podcast!

The other promos you can do on social media actually start before you record the podcast - for example, if it's an in-person recording, why not make an Instagram reel charting your journey to the recording, showing the studio etc. and have that ready to post either on the day of the recording or before it airs.

Take photos with the host to use on your Instagram stories - you can do this even if it's recorded via video call.

Think of what you enjoyed about that chat you had - what did you learn from it? What did you share? Use these to chat about either in stories or as a post caption.

And then when the podcast comes out, you can offer a collaboration, or agree to accept a collaboration post on Instagram with the podcast host, which means you get extra exposure to each other's audiences etc. and it makes it a stronger post with potentially greater reach.

And here's another HOT tip - if you do a collab post (or even if you don't) go on to the post that's been posted by the podcast or host, read the comments and like or reply to them. This is a great way of building engagement on the post itself but also of encouraging people in their audience to come over and join you on your page too.

So really think about the best way to use your social media to reach as many people as possible once the podcast airs.

Podcasts appearances can be very good for our credibility so the more ways we can make the most of them, the better.

See the next part for more on this…

Part 2. Maximising the podcast content

OK, we're sticking with ways to maximise the exposure of the podcast you've just appeared on.

So, we've talked a bit about social media.

But there's one big thing we can do when appearing on podcasts that not a lot of people do and it's a game changer.

A mentor of mine does this in a really super professional way but it can be done simply and cheaply too.

If you're recording a podcast via video call, an amazing thing to do is set up your phone, or a separate camera, to record just you.

So, say you're recording the podcast at your desk on your laptop - beside your laptop, set up your phone pointing just at you, and record the whole thing on your phone.

Why?

Well, this basically means you have the entire conversation recorded - but just at your end - which gives you loads of content to use. Because within that recording are a tonne of the key messages you want to share about your business, as well as your story potentially, and the knowledge you're sharing about whatever subject matter you're talking about.

This is so precious - because you can take that content you've recorded on your phone and break it down into short clips that can be used as reels, or stories, or maybe even on YouTube… all nuggets that you spoke about on that podcast which are now yours to use.

How cool is that!

NOTE: It's best not to use any of these clips from your phone until the podcast has aired, out of courtesy for the podcast host but once the episode is out, I would start sharing and sharing the shortened clips of the things I spoke about.

Honestly, if you can do this, it's a game changer as to how much use you can get from the content from just one podcast.

Other ways to use the content could be…

As an email to your email list - talking about some of the key messages you shared and linking to the podcast for your audience to listen

As a video on your own YouTube channel

As a freebie or lead magnet to help you attract more clients or customers for your business i.e. if you're a coach and on the podcast you shared 5 ways to never have to diet again or something like that, you could take that video, edit it, and create a lead magnet that offers people a free video on 5 ways to never have to diet again, all they have to do is fill in their email address to access the video, and that way you use it to build your email list.

If you have your own podcast, if the other podcast host agrees, you could post the episode as an episode of your own podcast too.

So there's lots of ways you can make the most of one podcast appearance if you really plan it!

How exciting!

Part 3. Learning as you go...

As with anything in life, in order to keep moving forward we need to keep learning as we go.

So to round off this process, it's good to measure a few things.

To start with, it might be worth noting your social media followers before the podcast airs, so you can see if you get new followers and how many after it's released. Similarly, you could monitor hits on your website in the same kind of before and after way.

Also as part of this process, I always like to think about what went well, what could have gone better and anything we would do differently next time.

Often we know these things, or we give them a fleeting moment of thought, but for me it's useful to spend 10/15mins just thinking through these questions and pulling out one or two key things to work on next time.

And this isn't about being critical of ourselves or finding fault - it's about learning and growing.

It could be something simple like maybe you want to mention your business name more during the podcast next time... or tell more stories about your clients or customers that really show off what you do.

Maybe you feel like you could have made more of it on social media.

Maybe you're proud of yourself for the way you told a story, or some advice you gave, or for simply showing up for your business in the first place.

Just mull it all over in a completely non-judgemental way and see where it takes you.

So ask yourself these questions…

-What went well?

-What could have gone better?

-What one or two things would I do differently next time?

And most of all give yourself a pat on the back because if you've been through this process and appeared as a podcast guest then you definitely deserve it!

CHAPTER 8

THE END

Summary and good luck

Right, we're done here!! If you've been through the entire book and reached this final chapter then well done - I know how tricky it can be to fit any kind of learning into your life!

I really hope you've taken everything you can out of it and like with any courses or programmes, the only way to actually benefit from them is to do the thing… and as someone much wiser than me once said, the only way to do the thing is to do the thing. Thinking about the thing isn't doing it, talking about the thing isn't doing it, preparing to do the thing isn't doing it… you have to actually do the thing to do the thing!

My farewell message is just really about getting out there and doing it. Remember how good you are at what you do. Remember why you want more people to know about your stuff and what you do.

Reach out prolifically to as many different kinds of podcasts as you can think of and find, and tailor your outreach to give yourself the best chance possible of getting yes.

Show up as your best self on the day, be prepared and be confident… and then make the most of the exposure afterwards through some of the ways I've outlined.

So you've got the step by step process and you can do it… believe me.

Get out there and get podcasting!! Thanks for reading and all the best.

The End

WORKSHEETS

Also available to download at **https://lindsayreidpr.com/resources/**

CHAPTER 1 - IT ALL STARTS WITH YOU

Worksheet 1 - YOUR GOAL

Once we know our 'why', our 'how' becomes clear…

Write down at least three goals you're trying to achieve through your podcast appearances…

1.

2.

3.

Write down WHY these matter to you (make as many points as you like)?

1.

2.

3.

Write down how you will feel when you achieve these outcomes?

1.

2.

3.

Write down how you want people to feel when they hear you on a podcast?

1.

2.

3.

Write down what actions you want people to take after hearing what you've got to say?

1.

2.

3.

Write down at least 3 things that your ideal customer wants?

1.

2.

3.

Write down at least 3 things that your ideal customer wants to avoid?

1.

2.

3.

Write down why your ideal customer needs you to show up for them? What happens if you're not there for them?

1.

2.

3.

Worksheet 2 - FINDING YOUR VOICE

Nobody knows more about your business than you!

Answer the following questions to help you find your voice!

What about me makes me the best person to talk about my business?

1.

2.

3.

What's the first thing I always tell people about my business… and why?

1.

If I only had one sentence to describe my business, and how it helps people, what would I say?

1.

What makes my business stand out from others and be that bit more extra special? (Name at least 3 things!)

1.

2.

3.

In what ways am I good at what I do? (Name at least 3 ways!)

1.

2.

3.

What are my main achievements in business (and/or life) over the past 5 years? (Write at least 10 things!)

1.

2.

3.

4.

5.

6.

7.

8.

9.

10.

Worksheet 3 - PASSION FOR WHAT YOU DO

Let your passion shine through!

Answer the following questions to help you rediscover and remember your passion for what you do!

What 5 things do I love most about my business?

1.

2.

3.

4.

5.

If my business didn't exist, in what ways would that impact my customers?

1.

2.

3.

Who are my happiest clients, how and why were they helped by my business and how did they feel? (Write as much as you can!)

1.

When have I felt my happiest during my business journey and what contributed to making me feel so happy?

1.

In what ways does my business improve my life and the lives of those around me? (Name at least 5 ways!)

1.

2.

3.

4.

5.

CHAPTER 4 - REACHING OUT TO GET A YES

Worksheet 4 - Be Specific

Sell your stats and tailor your outreach! You and your business are unique - now let's show why!

Facts and Figures (Complete as many of the below as you can....and add in more if you can think of more!)

- **xx** years 'experience in your chosen field/subject you want to talk about

- **xx** clients / customers supported (round to dozens, hundreds, thousands)

- **xx** followers on social media (again round up so if 2,350 followers say almost 2,500)

Write down previous podcasts you might have been on that supports your case to appear on the one you're reaching out to…

Note down any high profile people you've worked with that strengthens your case as a guest

Write down any awards you've won (then you can describe your business as award-winning which is super powerful)...

Make a note of any media coverage you've had in the past (i.e. as featured in / on)...

Note down anything else you feel strengthens your case to be on their show and demonstrates the value you'd bring to their audience…

CHAPTER 5 - PREPARING FOR YOUR PODCAST APPEARANCE

Worksheet 6 - Your Key Messages

Remember, you're there to share your messages with the world… now, go for it!

Write down all of the questions you think you might be asked (at least 10 questions)...

1.

2.

3.

4.

5.

6.

7.

8.

9.

10.

Write down your absolute non-negotiables… the things you ABSOLUTELY MUST tell the podcast audience (a maximum of 3)...

1.

2.

3.

Write down some examples of client success stories, things that happy clients have said, positive things that have been said about your business, times you've used your product...

1.

2.

3.

4.

5.

TEMPLATE EMAILS

Initial outreach email - Also available to download at https://lindsayreidpr.com/resources/

Hi **xxxxx (use the person's name if you know it)**.

I hope you're well. I love your podcast - it really helps me feel **xxxxx / I particularly enjoy xxxxxx (insert a couple of things you like about their podcast)**, thank you.

I actually wanted to put myself forward as a potential guest if that's ok!

My name is **xxxx (insert name)** and I **xxxxxxxx (insert your one sentence about what you do or what your business does)**.

My passion is shining a **light on / helping people with xxxx (share why you do what you do, why it's important to you)**

I would love to chat about this on your podcast as I know it's something that many of your audience will relate to and find interesting and helpful to hear.

My own story is one of **being a / struggling with / overcoming / learning / xxxxxxx (share some information about yourself as appropriate)**

I can also chat about… **(insert key themes you can share and discuss on their podcast)**

I have **xx years of experience (insert years of experience)** in supporting **hundreds/thousands of people (insert as appropriate)** in this way and **{OPTIONAL} have been named as xxxx (insert any awards you've won or DELETE IF NOT APPLICABLE).**

I'm building a strong, engaged community on social media with **xx followers across all channels (insert rough number of followers)** and a growing email list of **xxxx people (insert number if happy to or DELETE IF NOT APPLICABLE).**

I would love to share the conversation through my own channels to introduce my audience to you and the amazing work you do as well.

I also have my own podcast called **xxxxx (insert name) and would potentially love to have you as a guest on that too (DELETE IF NOT APPLICABLE)**

I really love the tone and style of conversations you have and together we would provide an interesting, valuable and entertaining podcast episode for your audience.

You can find more about me at **xxxxxx (insert social media/website links)**

Would this be of interest?

Thanks for your time,

xxxxxxx (sign off)

Follow-up email - also available to download at https://lindsayreidpr.com/resources/

Hi **xxxxx (use name if you know it)**,

I hope you're well. I sent you the below email **last month / a few weeks ago (delete as appropriate)** and just wondered if you've had a chance to consider it?

I can imagine you're very busy but I just think this would be a great podcast conversation for your audience if we can make it happen.

All of my details are in my previous email below.

Is this something you'd like to progress do you think?

Many thanks,

xxxxx (your name)

IMPORTANT LINKS

Chapter 2, Part 1
Your Podcasting Matching Worksheet - https://lindsayreidpr.com/resources/

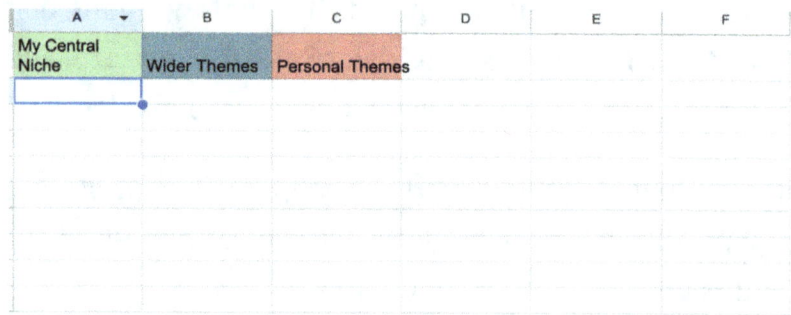

Chapter 3, Part 2
Video 1 - https://youtu.be/He_q8zY39wY
Video 2 - https://youtu.be/ii0X8nK7PQE

Chapter 4, Part 4
Your Podcast Tracking Worksheet - https://lindsayreidpr.com/resources/

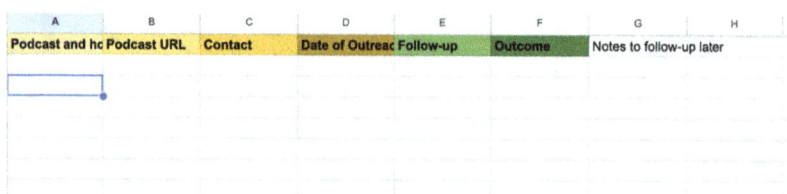

www.ingramcontent.com/pod-product-compliance
Lightning Source LLC
Chambersburg PA
CBHW071216240526
45470CB00018B/1887